# Productivity Tips - Getting More Out Of Life

Improve Your Personal Performance With Better Time Planning And Organization So You Can Live Your Life To The Fullest!

### Vanessa H. Tyson

Copyright © All Rights Reserved

We want to get more out of life and so we do more. Some days we get so overwhelmed with all the goals we've set up and all the many tasks we've lined up in order to attain those goals.

Swamped with doing so many things all at once and right away, we eventually tire our self out. The end result is demotivation. Stress and lack of clarity makes our path hard to organize and understand and so we fell less enthusiastic down the road than when we first began.

What to do first? How long to do it? What to do next? These questions call for us to manage our time and organize our activities so that we can get more things done and, therefore, get more out of life.

How many goals have you attained so far? How can you improve your personal performance? How can you do more and get them all done?

This book will help you:

1. Set daily goals
2. Determine your cycles of productiveness, and

3. Teach you lots of time-tested techniques for organization and time management

As a result, you can do more things in life and actually get all, well, at least a good number of them, done! Now, that's living life to the fullest!

# Disclaimer And Terms Of Use Agreement

The author and publisher have used their best efforts in preparing this book. The author and publisher make no representation or warranties with respect to the accuracy, applicability, fitness, or completeness of the contents of this book. The information contained in this book is strictly for educational purposes. Therefore, if you wish to apply ideas contained in this book, you are taking full responsibility for your actions.

Every effort has been made to accurately represent this product and its potential. However, there is no guarantee that you will improve in any way using the techniques and ideas in these materials. Examples in these materials are not to be interpreted as a promise or guarantee of anything. Self-help and improvement potential is entirely dependent on the person using our product, ideas and techniques.

Your level of improvement in attaining the results claimed in our materials depends on the time you devote to the program, ideas and techniques mentioned and knowledge and various skills. Since these factors differ according to individuals, we cannot guarantee your success or improvement level. Nor are we responsible for any of your actions.

Many factors will be important in determining your actual results and no guarantees are made that you will achieve results similar to ours or anybody else's, in fact no guarantees are made that you will achieve any results from our ideas and techniques in our material.

The author and publisher disclaim any warranties (express or implied), merchantability, or fitness for any particular purpose. The author and publisher shall in no event be held liable to any party for any direct, indirect, punitive, special, incidental or other consequential damages arising directly or indirectly from any use of this material, which is provided "as is", and without warranties.

As always, the advice of a competent professional should be sought.

The author and publisher do not warrant the performance, effectiveness or applicability of any sites listed or linked to in this book.

# Table of Contents

Disclaimer And Terms Of Use Agreement ................... 3
Table of Contents ............................................................ 5
Foreword ........................................................................... 6
Chapter 1: Dump It Or Do It ......................................... 8
   Setting Daily Goals ..................................................... 9
Chapter 2: Peak Cycles Of Productiveness ................ 11
Chapter 3: No Communication Times and Micro-Mileposts ......................................................................... 14
Chapter 4: Time Framing ............................................. 17
Chapter 5: Pacing and Clear The Clutter .................... 21
Chapter 6: Bust Procrastination and 60 Second Decisions......................................................................... 24
Chapter 7: Accountability and Visualize .................... 27
Chapter 8: Reward and Plan......................................... 30
Chapter 9: Assign and Expand Your Interests........... 33
Chapter 10: Hunch and Optimize................................ 36
Wrapping Up .................................................................. 40

# Foreword

Heuristics are conventions specified to help you solve problems.

When an issue is large or complex, and the optimal solution is unclear, employing a heuristic lets you start making progress towards a resolution even though you can't envision the entire path from your starting point.

Suppose your goal is to drive to the store, but there's no road to follow. An illustration of a heuristic would be: Head directly toward the store till you reach an obstacle you can't cross. Whenever you contact such an obstacle, follow it around to the right till you're able to head toward the store again.

This isn't the most levelheaded or comprehensive heuristic, but in a lot of cases it will work just fine, and you'll finally reach the store.

Heuristics don't ensure you'll find the optimum solution, nor do they broadly guarantee a resolution at all. But they do a beneficial enough job of solving particular types of problems to be of real value.

Their strength is that they break the impasse of indecision and get you into action. As you take action you start to explore the solution space, which heightens your understanding of the issue. As you acquire knowledge about the issue, you can make course corrections along the way, gradually bettering your chances of finding a resolution. If you attempt to solve an issue you don't initially know how to figure out, you'll often work out a solution as you go, one you never could have imagined till you began moving. This is particularly true with creative work like product development.

Often you don't even recognize precisely what you're attempting to build till you begin building it.

Heuristics have a lot of practical applications, and among my favorite areas of application is personal productivity. Productivity heuristics are behavioral rules (a few general, some situation-specific) that may help us get matters done more efficiently.

# Chapter 1: Dump It Or Do It

The most effective way to click a task is to get rid of it. If it doesn't need to be done, get it off your to do list.

A central dogma of many time management and personal productivity systems is that you need to expend more of your time doing those activities that are more crucial for reaching your goals, and less time doing those matters that are more insignificant. You must invest most of your time each week doing what you do best, and let other people do what they do best. Assigning some of your tasks to other people (maybe more qualified) individuals can free up your time and energy to follow up on your highest priority goals.

For example, you may choose to hire an accountant instead of preparing your taxes yourself, thereby freeing up a couple of hours of your time and perhaps reducing stress. Naturally, each of us has to work out the value of one's time versus the economic cost of hiring somebody to do yard work, home repairs, and so on.

## Setting Daily Goals

Without a clear focus, it's too easy to buckle under to distractions. Set targets for every day beforehand. Decide what you'll do; then do it.

We often discuss our goals as if they're nothing but dreams. Actually, we can accomplish goals on a daily basis. Daily goals contribute to weekly goals. Weekly goals add to monthly goals. Monthly goals add to-- you guessed it--yearly goals. With some prevision and planning, our goals can be something we accomplish day in and day out. Here's how to begin.

Arrive at a list of goals every single day. Even if you foresee a slow day, it's still a beneficial idea to set goals for yourself. The sooner you assume the habit of setting daily goals, the earlier you'll get into the habit of meeting them.

Keep your every day goal lists in one place. You are able to utilize a spiral notebook, a PDA or your computer's calendar program.

Keeping your goals in one place lets you look over the lists from days and weeks passed, which makes it simple for you to see how systematically you're meeting your goals.

Be honest about your daily goals. A goal like "Make $2,000 before 5p.m." is undefined and unrealistic, but a goal like "Network with 4 clients" is totally attainable--and just may help you work toward that $2,000.

Picture your daily goals as the "building blocks" of your weekly and monthly goals. For instance, if you prefer to send marketing material to 10 prospective clients by the end of the week, make it your goal to send out material to 2 prospective clients per work day.

# Chapter 2: Peak Cycles Of Productiveness

To shoot down procrastination learn to undertake your most obnoxious task first thing in the morning rather than detaining it till later in the day. This little triumph will set the tone for a really productive day.

Consider why you procrastinate: Are you afraid of flunking at the task? Are you a perfectionist and only willing to start working after every little element is in place? Are you easily disturbed? Break up a big, hard project into several smaller pieces. Tackle each piece individually. Set deadlines for completion.

Attempt assigning yourself modest deadlines ' for instance, commit to reading a particular number of pages in the next hour. Work in little blocks of time rather than in long stretches. Try working in one – to two hour spurts, letting yourself have a small break after each stretch.

Do away with distractions or move to a place where you are able to concentrate. Switch off the TV, the phone ringer, the radio and anything else that may keep you from your task.

Identify your apex cycles of productiveness, and schedule your most crucial jobs for those times. Work at minor tasks during your non-peak times.

What time of day is your most productive? This question was posed in a poll. So while there seems to be no fixed time of day that's the most productive for everybody, the recent poll of 181 individuals did supply some insights into who gets the most done when. Here, then, are some insights into people's most productive hours.

In the total results, thirty-six percent of those reviewed said that the morning between nine and eleven was their most productive hours.

In 2nd place was early morning, when thirty-one percent of those who answered said their productivity was at its peak.

The lowest time for productivity was between twelve and two p.m., with only six percent of respondents stating this was their most productive hours. A mere nine percent said the evening between 7:30 and 10 was their most generative. "

So what does all this mean to you, and how can you employ it in your daily life? Here's the 2 suggestions about how to find and capitalize on their most productive time of day.

Start by locating your power times. Are you an early riser who takes on your morning to-do list with all the zest of a bear eating honey?

Maybe you're a night owl and zip through your most urgent projects at 11 p.m.? Either way, knowing and capitalizing on your natural energy patterns — your power times — will help you be at your most productive by utilizing these times to tackle the projects you find most ambitious.

# Chapter 3: No Communication Times and Micro-Mileposts

Priorities

Apportion uninterruptible blocks of time for unaccompanied work where you must focus. Schedule light, interruptible jobs for your open communication time periods and more ambitious projects for your no communication periods.

1st, cut down disruptions You can't truly begin adding more productive activities to your work schedule till you free yourself from productivity-sapping interruptions. Try these strategies.

1. Resolve problems before they occur. Start by analyzing interruptions. Are there frequent time wasters that could be avoided with a little more upfront planning?

2. Group like activities. If at all conceivable, ask people to reschedule their communication with you during the same period. In that way, you are able to have several productive hours before being interrupted.

Likewise, attempt to block out particular times in your day to return calls. Unless it's a real emergency—which are few, a client isn't going to have a problem with getting a message that says "I will call you back between 11 and noon this morning." And grouping all my call returns together lets me concentrate on other things instead of constantly dropping everything to respond to a call.

3. Schedule disruptions. Appropriate particular times during the day—around lunch, for instance—when you're available to answer colleagues' questions, catch up with friends, or talk to your children.

Apply this even to your family, unless it's an emergency.

Micro-Mileposts

When you start a task, name the target you must reach before you are able to quit working. For instance, when working on a book, you may decide not to get up till you've written at least a thousand words. Hit your target regardless what.

You are able to think of goal setting as a process that helps you to decide precisely what it is that you want, and then to systematically do what you need to do in order to get it.

It's a process that helps you center your time and energy on your most crucial targets, produce strategies and plans to reach them, take action, and make adjustments as necessary till you reach them.

# Chapter 4: Time Framing

Using Time Periods

Give yourself a fixed period of time, like half-hour, to make a dent in a job. Don't worry about how far you get. Simply put in the time.

Time framing is an easy time management technique I use often. Let's suppose you have a fixed deadline for a fresh product you need to release, like a new e-book. You must have a fresh version ready by a particular date. So you'll likely use time framing for your developing cycle, meaning that you do the finest job you can inside the time available. What fresh material you can implement is totally ascertained by the time frame. Falling away from the schedule is plainly not an option, so if you drop behind, you must cut features.

In terms of managing your own undertakings, time framing may be a helpful strategy.

1st, let's say you would like to get something done, but there's a chance it could end up taking far more time than it's worth as it's the sort of chore where you may exhibit perfectionist dispositions. So you give yourself a particular amount of time, which you won't go over, and you simply do the best job you are able to inside that time.

The 2nd way is when I've a chore or project that I want to finish, but I don't truly know where to start, or it seems like it's going to be a while before I can complete a meaningful lump. Or perhaps it's something I find truly boring and would have an inclination to dilly-dally on. Then I use time framing to merely commit to working on the job for a given time period to make a scratch in it. I commonly utilize a period in the range of thirty -one hundred twenty minutes. I expel any concern about reaching a certain milestone inside that time — I merely commit to putting in the time, no matter how far I get.

A side effect of this last technique is that I'll often wind up working much longer than I originally designated. If I commit to working at a boring task for just half-hour, it's easy to get going because I've given myself license to stop after only half-hour. But once I've overcome that inertia and am now centered on the job, ninety minutes might pass before I even feel the desire to quit.

Wake Early

Arise early in the morning, like at 5am, and go directly to work on your most crucial task. You are able to frequently get more done before 8am than most individuals do in a day.

The different ways you are able to start getting up early daily.

**Method One - Gradual Reduction**

Sleeping is like an addiction and like any addiction you are able to gradually move away from it. If you are a heavy sleeper you may want to begin gradually arising earlier and earlier everyday until you accomplish your target time.

This technique has the advantage that you won't have to bond right into the early mornings. However, I've found a lot of individuals are not as successful with this technique as it's too slow and gives you too much time to drop-off track.

However, I've found that some other individuals truly like this approach. The gradual change is softer and often leads them to some spontaneous change where they feel they're ready to tip it all the way to a very early start.

## Method Two - Quick Change

If your reasons are beneficial enough and your will is strong enough the best way to arise early is to start tomorrow. Set the clock for the correct time and get up regardless what. Your mind will try all sorts of games with you but you must dismiss it and stay strong and in charge.

I've found this to be the best technique. After two weeks it became normal. After a month I couldn't sleep in after 5am even when I wanted to. It had become habit.

I personally believe this is the best way to wake early. Promise yourself you'll get up at a particular time and then do it. Don't change for anything, no matter what.

# Chapter 5: Pacing and Clear The Clutter

Designedly pick up the pace, and try to move a little faster than usual.

Talk faster. Walk faster. Type quicker. Read quicker. Finish sooner.

Improve the quality of your sleep. When your sleep is optimized, you could actually sleep less, but have more energy than you've had before, when you slept longer. Begin by reducing the amount of caffeine you get during the day, particularly in the evening.

Remember, caffeine isn't present only in coffee, but likewise in soda, tea and chocolate, to name a few. Also, go to bed only when you really need to, and not only because of a schedule.

Be more active. Have you noticed that the times that you're most tired are the times that you've no reason to be? You know what I'm discussing. You just woke up from a long nap and since then all you've been doing is lay on the coach, but still, all you want to do is rest, and sleep.

It's a bit of a paradox, but when your activity level is really low, so is your energy level. Begin moving yourself. If exercising is a bit much for you, the least you can do is stretch. Likewise, climb the stairs rather than taking the elevator, walk those few yards to the market instead of driving to it, play with your dog, or your youngsters. A couple of changes to your diet could greatly increase your energy level. You should probably begin by doubling the amount of water you drink each day. Also, rather than starting your day with coffee and a muffin, how about some cereal and orange juice?

Organize your thoughts. If you've too much on your mind and prefer not to begin thinking of all the things you have to do, it's time to write it down. Write everything that comes to your mind, things to do, things to consider, things that bother you. You'd likely realize soon enough, that things aren't as bad as you thought. Acknowledge your inner dialog. Do you talk to yourself like a parent talks to a child?

You're grownup now. It's time to change the way you consider tasks and responsibilities. Rather than thinking "YOU have to do this", think- "I wish to do this because..." and give yourself a really good reason why.

Clear The Clutter

Cut down stress by cultivating a relaxing, clutter-free workspace.

The first time you see your workspace daily, you should feel good about it. It should be attractive to you. Truly it should be your favorite place in the entire building, house, or campus. If you're in your workspace right now, please step outdoors for a minute, and then re-enter it while paying close attention to your sensations.

What's the very first emotional reaction you can detect? Do you feel strained? Overpowered? Blasé? Apathetic? Focused? Peaceful? Is this an emotion you experience often while working?

Now pick the emotion you want to feel, and experiment with different visual elements to see how they change your feelings. Try fresh furniture, photos, posters, mirrors, flowers, bric-a-bracs, toys, statues, rugs, artwork, crystals, etc. If you've the necessary control, you are able to also tweak the lighting in your workspace to produce the right type of mood.

# Chapter 6: Bust Procrastination and 60 Second Decisions

Bust procrastination by taking action instantly after setting a goal, even if the action isn't perfectly planned. You are able to always correct course along the way.

Among the most crucial things you can do for yourself is to get organized. Make lists, take a class in organization, or buy an organizer. Do whatever works for you. One warning: follow the KISS principle (Keep it Simple, Stupid). If your organization system is too perplexed, it will become just another chore to avoid.

- Make a list of what needs to get executed. This can be listed in no particular order and will give you a handle on just what you need to achieve.

- Prioritize these. My way of arranging this is by deadlines. I arrange them in order of when they're due. You might also decide to rank them by how important it is to get them done. For instance, paying your bills on time might be more significant to you than cleaning out your closets. Do that first.

- Get yourself a calendar with room to write notes in. make pages with dates for long-run planning and also keep a separate list to transfer short-term goals to.

- Take what's at the top of your priority list and ascertain how long it will take to achieve it. If it's a fast task, put that down to be done the current day. If it will take a longer time, divide it into littler tasks to be spread over several days. Write this in your calendar with particular dates for achieving each. Include your deadline for culmination of this task on your calendar too.

- Keep filling your calendar till you've a time set aside to do each item while still meeting your deadlines. Be deliberate to not overbook yourself and allow plenty of time for delays. This will let you feel confident that you can achieve all you need to in the time you have. Now you are able to relax and work on one item at a time without feeling you have to do it all at once.

## 60 Second Decisions

Once you've the information you need to make a decision, begin a timer and give yourself just 60 seconds to make the actual decision.

Take a whole minute to waver and second-guess yourself all you want, but come out the other end with a clear-cut choice. Once your decision is attained, take some sort of action to set it in motion.

When we view choices as being more than just paths — as being originative statements of self-expression — particular decisions become much easier to make. You might say to yourself, "This path isn't going to be simple, but I know this is the right way to go because it's who I am." Or you might resolve, "regardless how I try to represent this to myself, I know that at heart this isn't who I am. This just isn't me."

It's really important to separate this evaluation step from the act of summoning the bravery to act on this knowledge. It's OK to acknowledge you're in a place you don't want to be, even when you lack the ability to do anything about it right now. The bravery to act comes later.

# Chapter 7: Accountability and Visualize

**See and Do**

Tell other people of your commitments, since they'll help hold you accountable.

Take time to consider if keeping the promise in question is executable. Being realistic and not going too much above and beyond what you're capable of will help you keep your promise successfully.

Note the steps called for to keep your promise. These could be steps which are obvious and necessary, or steps like reminding yourself to bring fruit to work so you are able to supplement healthy food for nicotine when you are trying to quit smoking. Keep a record of your progress. You're more probable to keep your promise when you write it down. Make notes about your progress. If parts of the plan aren't functioning, then make alterations. Communicate any troubles you have. This way you can get assistance, if necessary.

## Visualize

Visualize your goal as already achieved. Put yourself into a state of actually being there. Make it actual in your mind, and you'll soon see it in your reality.

Discover a quiet, comfortable place where you won't be distracted for a few minutes. Close your eyes and count backwards from seven to one, letting yourself unwind as you go. When you get to the number 1, find yourself walking on a path. It could be in the forest, through a field, along the beach-wherever YOUR magic relaxation spot is. Know that this decidedly is YOUR path. At the end of the path is the matter you want to visualize. Could be a new home, a new job, a fresh relationship, or something in the intangible realm like better listening skills. When you see that visualization- take in the particulars. Truly enjoy this, get all of your senses involved, and get your emotions tangled in the experience. Big key: feel and hold the exhilaration of what you're visualizing. And then let it go. Send your petition out into the universe. Consider your request floating in a balloon, magnetically drawing in to you the tools you need in order for the visualization to materialize.

Pay attention to the clues that crop up in your life- people you meet, articles you read, conversations you overhear- these will lead you closer to creation. Look out for an "iron grip." It's difficult for things to flow to you if you're holding onto your want with such a tight grip that avenues don't become evident. Greatest key of all: Note the disconnect between what you visualized and what you actually feel afterward, either right after or as the day gets on. Your negative ego may crop up with snide comments like, "Oh, that's just not possible for me to have a nice home." "Who do you think you are?" "You don't merit that." "That's not your path, it's way too nice." Catch those beliefs, listen to the whispers, and write them down. Ask yourself what you'd have to do to alter that limiting belief. Write down the stale belief and burn it in a safe place. Write down the fresh belief and display where you are able to see it. Return into the visualization again.

# Chapter 8: Reward and Plan

**Reward Yourself**

Give yourself frequent rewards for accomplishment. See a film, book a professional massage, or spend a day at a funfair.

It's important to reward yourself when you accomplish or achieve your goals. This will inspire you to do more and go the extra mile to accomplish your top goals in life.

When you've completed or accomplished one of your goals, treat yourself, you don't have to spend a lot of money. Just be creative. You can treat yourself to a bubble bath with candles and wine or to sit down with a good book.

Consider all the little things you could do to reward yourself for any effort done to complete your goals. Make a list of what you'd like and do something for yourself. It doesn't have to cost any money. Attend that workshop on arts and crafts you always wanted to do. Or begin meditating; there are perpetual possibilities for you to enrich your life further.

Make certain you apply this reward system after accomplishing each of your goals.

**One Month Plan**

Identify a fresh habit you'd like to form, and commit to adhering to it for just thirty days. A temporary commitment is much easier to keep than a permanent one.

Let's say you want to begin a new habit like an exercise program or quit a bad habit like sucking on cigarettes. We all know that getting rolling and sticking with the new habit for a couple of weeks is the hard part. Once you've overpowered inertia, it's much easier to keep on.

Yet we often psyche ourselves out of getting rolling by mentally thinking of the change as something permanent — before we've even started. It seems too overpowering to think about making a huge change and sticking with it daily for the rest of your life when you're still accustomed to doing the opposite. The more you consider the change as something permanent, the more you stay put.

But what if you thought of making the change only temporarily — say for thirty days — and then you're free to go back to your old habits?

That doesn't seem so difficult any longer. Exercise daily for just thirty days, then quit. Keep a neatly organized desk for thirty days, and then let up. Read for an hour a day for thirty days, and then go back to watching television.

It still calls for a bit of discipline and commitment, but not nearly so much as making a lasting change. Any perceived deprivation is only temporary. You are able to count down the days to freedom. And for at least thirty days, you'll gain some advantage.

Now if you really complete a 30-day trial, what's going to happen? 1st, you'll go far enough to institute it as a habit, and it will be easier to sustain than it was to begin it. Second, you'll break the addiction of your old habit during this time. Third, you'll have thirty days of success behind you, which will give you higher confidence that you can keep going. And fourth, you'll gain thirty days worth of results, which will give you practical feedback on what you are able to expect if you keep on, putting you in a better place to make informed long-run decisions.

# Chapter 9: Assign and Expand Your Interests

**Assign**

Convince somebody else to do it for you.

Being able to delegate effectively is essential to the success of your business or the running of your household. When you realize that you cannot do everything exclusively, it is time to begin delegating. Wait till you see how much more can get done with the help of other people.

Make a list of all jobs that need to be accomplished. A list will help you see how much needs to be done. Group the jobs by the required date of culmination. Begin with jobs that need to be done 1st and finish with jobs that don't have to be done straight off. Evaluate the skills of the individuals who are assisting with the project.

Comprehending everyone's skill sets is crucial in delegating effectively. Assign tasks based on skills and interests. Giving individuals jobs that they like produces better results. Be clear on what you want done. Convey both verbally and in writing the tasks to be finished. Give specifics if essential. When applicable, allow the individual some freedom in how they finish the tasks. Compliment a job well done. This encouragement is crucial for motivation in future projects.

As well, offer critiques when necessary but privately.

**Expand Your Interests**

Sign up for martial arts, begin a blog, or link up with a self-improvement group. You'll frequently come across ideas in one field that can boost your execution in another.

There are a few basic ways to get motivated to try and learn new things to expand one:

In the case of learning and expanding your hobbies and interests you may want to ascertain what it is you want out of that hobby or from that education. Do you want to be a doctor; do you want to aid individuals? What about becoming a professional athlete or an Olympian? And, there is no shame in wanting to make millions of dollars if that's your goal.

Once you know what end result you want it's easier to set up goals and get motivated to accomplish them.

There are many sources for finding and determining how to expand your interests and what steps you need to make to get there. Finding the right teachers, schools, and mentors are all important.

Naturally, TV and the Internet can also be good sources of learning and expanding interests. The Net offers such an expanse of knowledge and opportunity for growth and learning. And, although much of TV is brainless there are definitely thought provoking and educational programs as well. Both are a matter of just seeking out those things that you're interested in learning.

# Chapter 10: Hunch and Optimize

**Trust Better**

Go with your gut hunch. It's likely right.

The mind asks questions. If you're nervous about a state of affairs and hear yourself asking questions that begin with; What if? How? But? And Why? Then you know your mind is taking over. Take a deep breath and ask yourself," What am I afraid will happen?" Then be willing for the unsought to take place.

Frequently, if you'll just be willing to face whatever happens, the outcome isn't as severe as your mind has created it to be. As a matter of fact, you may be pleased with the result. There's no anxiety with the Gut. No emotional component. The answers are always pragmatic.

It is not necessary to find a calm room, meditate, chant, stand on one's head, do a fire walk or convert to a vegetarian to key into the voice of your Gut. Once you're open to the Gut's message, getting guidance becomes effortless. It merely requires willingness to let go of the fear and doubt of the mind, and trust that inner voice.

Occasionally this message is shrieking within you, yet you're clouded. You plug your ears, and close your eyes, you don't want to let go of previous habits. Even though they have not worked, they're comfortable. Trusting your Gut will move you to the place you're meant to be.

**Optimize**

Discover the processes you utilize most often, and write them down step-by-step. Re- author them on paper for greater efficiency. Then apply and test your improved processes. Occasionally we just can't see what's right in front of us till we examine it under a microscope.

Whatever your goal is (to lose weight, to run a 5K, to gain muscle strength) create a mental picture of yourself having already accomplished it. What will you look like, feel like, and move like when you've achieved that goal? Living as if you're already there makes realizing your vision something you center on daily.

Understanding who you are as an individual, and why you make the selections you make, is so crucial. Don't work against your natural tendencies- work with them! If you are a walker, don't try to force yourself into becoming a long-distance runner. If you are a social butterfly, take a new fitness class with a friend, or if you favor solo exercise, examine a new Pilates DVD at home.

Little things can make major shifts in life. Attempt substituting half of your usual morning OJ with carbonated water or try your usual sandwich with one less slice of bread and more lettuce alternatively today. Swap out your favorite television program for a half hour with a book that you've been waiting to read. Offer to take your friend's kids for the afternoon so that she has a couple of hours of "me" time, and then she may return the favor. Over time, these tiny steps can produce major results.

When you know you've been good to yourself, treat yourself! Find a reward that inspires you- a new pair of sneakers or workout outfit, a new music CD for your walk or pamper your feet with a pedicure for all of your efforts. You may be surprised - that gold-star, pat-on-the-back goes a long way towards helping you remain motivated.

We all need a boost now and then, and occasionally the best way to get it is by doing LESS, not MORE. Resist the urge to push yourself to your limits, and try going the other way. Examine a yoga class, treat yourself to a massage or simply sit still and just center on your breath for 10 minutes today.

# Wrapping Up

Individuals can get engrossed in the details of their lives and chase the next big thing without finding time to complete the projects they previously started. When faced with all of their incomplete projects, they often become deluged and start to procrastinate. You'll find that their productivity decreases and they don't produce the results or environment you're used to seeing. What are the things on your list of things that need to get done?

After using the tools in this book not only should you see an increase in productivity, but you should get more results - better results. Your motivation and drive will also increase as you reap the rewards of positive results.

Made in the USA
Middletown, DE
15 April 2016